Granny Mai Eats the Rainbow

By Oonagh Armstrong

Illustrated by C Little & J Leneghan

Created by The Johnny Magory Co. Ltd

First published 2022 by The Johnny Magory Company Limited.

Ballynafagh, Prosperous, Naas, Co. Kildare, Ireland

Text and illustrations © Oonagh Armstrong

The right of Oonagh Armstrong

to be identified as the Author of the work has been asserted by them in accordance with the Copyright Acts.

All rights reserved. No part of this publication may be reproduced, distributed, or transmitted in any form or by any means, including photocopying, recording or other electronic or mechanical methods, without the prior written permission of the publisher, except in the case of brief quotations embodied in critical reviews and certain other non-commercial uses permitted by copyright law.

Oonagh Armstrong created this story and book following a six-week writing course during 2021 with Emma-Jane Leeson of The Johnny Magory Company Ltd.

For the most amazing little boy, Alex

Charlie loves his granny,

She has superpowers you see.

She's the oldest person in the world

And is always so full of glee.

You see Granny Mai is ninety-nine,

But looks so young and strong.

Charlie is sure no one else could be that age,

Or would ever live that long.

Charlie talks all day about Granny,

How she is funny and oh so kind.

She loves to hike up mountains,

A crazier granny, you will not find!

She has superhuman strength

And runs at the speed of light!

Her limbs are like Stretch Armstrong's

And she is not afraid of heights.

Granny is a computer genius

And can read your mind, they say.

She even owns a superwoman cape!

Oh how Charlie loves Granny Mai.

She has supersonic vision,

Knows you inside out, from your head to your toe.

And she must have eyes at the back of her head,

Because if you are naughty, she will always know.

She's a pro in the kitchen,

A master chef we all agree.

She can whip up a roast dinner in three seconds flat,

And makes the **BEST** cup of tea.

She knows EVERY answer,

To EVERY question she is asked!

She has read EVERY book,

Because she can read them oh so fast.

Charlie often wondered,

How Granny got so tall and strong,

And what was the secret to all her superpowers,

And how she lived so long?

"It's really simple Charlie,"
Said Granny Mai one day,
"You must EAT THE RAINBOW,
Then strong and mighty you will stay."

"Eat the rainbow?"
Charlie was confused!
"Come on," said Granny Mai,
"I'll show you all the tricks I've used."

Off outside they ventured,

and a colourful rainbow they found,

"Lets go Charlie," said Granny Mai,

"I'm going to show you around."

Red will give you strength,

Peppers, tomatoes, strawberries and grapes.

These are the magic ingredients,

That will earn you superman capes.

"Eat the rainbow every day,

Eat the rainbow," said Granny Mai.

Orange is the magic that will make you grow so tall,

Carrots, pumpkin, squash and peach,

If these are the foods that you eat,

Well the sky you will indeed reach.

"Eat the rainbow every day,

Eat the rainbow," said Granny Mai.

Yellow makes a clever brain,

Cantaloupe, pineapple, squash and banana.

This is the secret Charlie,

To help you be as clever as your nana!!

"Eat the rainbow every day,

Eat the rainbow," said Granny Mai.

Charlie always eat your Greens,

Broccoli, peas, spinach and kale.

Important advice, this is my dear,

And then through life you will sail.

"Eat the rainbow every day,

Eat the rainbow," said Granny Mai.

Blue will help you at school each day,

Figs, blueberry, blackberry and prune.

These sweets from nature we must eat,

To be full of health from morning till noon!

"Eat the rainbow every day,

Eat the rainbow," said Granny Mai.

Finally my dear, Indigo and Violet,

Elderberries, cabbage, aubergine and plum.

These will give you energy for days,

And now to the end of the rainbow we have come.

"Eat the rainbow every day,

Eat the rainbow," said Granny Mai.

Charlie was amazed!

He had never known,

How simple it was to be like Granny,

Well his mind was just blown!

The rainbow Charlie will eat,

From this day on,

To have superpowers like

Granny Mai,

And hopefully live that long.

About the Author

Oonagh Armstrong is a Primary School Teacher and a Nutritional Therapist based in Castlebar, Co. Mayo. The idea for this book came from a combination of her two passions: children's education and nutrition education.

She became inspired to start writing because she saw a need for more fictional books to inspire healthy eating in children. The hope for this book is to help parents and teachers alike, to encourage children to eat the rainbow and become educated on the importance of good nutrition.

Oonagh can be found @oonagharmstrongnutrition on Facebook and Instagram.

L - #0258 - 031122 - C24 - 210/148/1 [3] - CB - DID3413770